savoury & sweet
Crumbles
with friends

Recipes by Camille Le Foll
Photographs by Akiko Ida

HACHETTE Illustrated

contents

Tips and advice	4
Apple crumble	6
Red fruit crumble	8
Quince crumble	10
Morello cherry crumble	12
Spicy pear crumble	14
Black fruit crumble	16
Lemon crumble	18
Quick red fruit crumble	20
Nectarine crumble	22
English summer crumble	24
Tropical crumble	26
Spicy crumble	28
Cheesecake crumble	30
Apricot and lavender crumble	32

Sweet spiced tomato crumble   34

Winter fruits crumble   36

Dark chocolate crumble   38

White chocolate crumble   40

Pear, banana and chocolate crumble   42

Iced coffee crumble   44

Savoury tomato crumble   46

Courgette crumble   48

Pumpkin crumble   50

Spring vegetable crumble   52

Mediterranean crumble   54

Crumble Indian style   56

Oriental crumble   58

Moroccan crumble   60

Chicken liver crumble   62

tips and advice

Chantilly cream

250 ml (8 fl oz) whipping cream (chill for approximately 2 hours before whipping) or thick crème fraîche

Beat with an electric beater, allowing as much air as possible to enter the cream. Begin slowly then build up speed gradually. Once the cream is nicely frothed and full of air bubbles (do not overbeat), add about 15 g (½ oz) of vanilla sugar, or icing sugar and vanilla essence to taste, or any desired flavourings, such as cinnamon, alcohol, orange juice or coffee essence.

The thick crème fraîche found in supermarkets has usually been thickened artificially with lactic fermenting agents that do not allow it to froth up well. It is therefore best to use whipping cream (fresh or UHT). For a more pronounced flavour, try to get hold of traditional thick crème fraîche and add a little ice or milk before whipping.

Custard

Serves 8
Makes about 1 litre (1¾ pints)

750 ml (1¼ pints) milk
1–2 vanilla pods, split in half lengthwise
6 egg yolks
100 g (3½ oz) caster sugar

Bring the milk up to boiling point along with the vanilla pods. Remove from the heat and leave to steep for 10 minutes. Scrape out the seeds from the pods and mix them into the milk.

Beat the egg yolks with the sugar until frothy and very pale yellow.

Gradually pour in the hot milk, beating continuously. Pour the mixture back into the pan and thicken over very gentle heat, stirring continuously with a wooden spoon until the custard coats the back of the spoon and the surface is no longer frothy.

Remove from the heat and continue to stir for 2 minutes before allowing to cool.

Brown sugars

Demerara sugar: crystallized brown sugar extracted from sugar cane. Clear in colour, it has a slight flavour of rum.

Soft brown sugar: extracted from sugar cane or beet. This sugar is softer in texture than Demerara sugar and is available in two versions: a light brown sugar with a subtle flavour and a dark brown version with a strong flavour.

Muscovado sugar: obtained through evaporation of the cane juice. It is completely unrefined and so has retained most of its vitamins and minerals, in particular magnesium, phosphorus and iron. Dark in colour, it comes in small, unevenly sized crystals, owing to the residue and impurities contained in it, and has a very strong flavour, which gives it its name.

Excess juice

Unfortunately, some fruit (and also some vegetables) give off a lot of juice when they are cooking, which can make the crumble soggy. However, certain ingredients can be added that act as excellent moisture absorbers: a tiny quantity of tapioca or ground rice will absorb the excess juice released by fruit, while semolina can be used for savoury dishes. Some biscuits, especially sponge fingers are also very effective and can be crumbled between the fruit and the crumble topping.

Biscuits

Great fun can be had making original and delicious crumbles using biscuits or cakes, such as shortbread, ginger-bread or spiced loaf (crumbled or toasted), digestive biscuits, ginger thins, macaroons, etc.

The art of crumbling

Generally, it is always best to make the crumble mixture by hand, not with an electric mixer, which has a tendency to crush the ingredients.

The best method, although by no means the fastest, is to rub together the well-chilled butter and flour with a soft, light touch, without kneading the mixture, then stir in the sugar and any other ingredients. If you have time, leave the mixture to stand for a while in the refrigerator before spreading over the filling.

Apple crumble

filling

6–7 cooking apples, peeled, cored and cut into pieces

50 g (2 oz) butter

topping

220 g (7½ oz) plain flour

pinch of salt

200 g (7 oz) unsalted butter, diced

200 g (7 oz) caster sugar

Preheat the oven to 180°C (350°F), gas mark 4.

Brown the apples in a pan in the butter.

Prepare the crumble topping by putting the flour, salt and butter in a bowl and rubbing them together lightly with your finger tips to form large crumbs. Add the sugar and mix well to disperse evenly. Spread a thin layer of crumble at the bottom of an ovenproof dish, cover with the apples and sprinkle the rest of the crumble on top.

Bake in the preheated oven for 40–50 minutes, or until the crumble topping is golden brown.

Red fruit crumble

filling

700 g (1½ lb) mixed red fruit (raspberries, redcurrants, blackberries, blackcurrants, blueberries, etc), cleaned and prepared. (Remove the stalks from the redcurrants and blackcurrants.)

30–50 g (1–2 oz) caster sugar, depending on the acidity of the fruit

1 tablespoon tapioca or ground rice

topping

170 g (6 oz) plain flour

pinch of salt

100 g (3½ oz) unsalted butter, diced

170 g (6 oz) caster sugar

Preheat the oven to 180°C (350°F), gas mark 4.

Mix the fruit together with the sugar and spread evenly in an ovenproof dish. Sprinkle with the tapioca or ground rice

Prepare the crumble topping by putting the flour, salt and butter into a bowl and rubbing them together lightly with your finger tips to form large crumbs. Add the sugar and mix well to disperse evenly.

Spread the topping evenly over the fruit filling.

Bake in the preheated oven for 25–30 minutes, until the topping is golden brown.

Serve warm with vanilla ice cream.

Quince crumble

filling

500 g (1 lb) quinces,
peeled, cored and
quartered

50 g (2oz) caster sugar

500 g (1 lb) dessert apples,
e.g. Cox's orange pippins,
peeled, cored and chopped

500 g (1 lb) soft, ripe pears,
peeled, cored and chopped

1 tablespoon essence of
rosewater

topping

200 g (7 oz) plain flour

175 g (6 oz) butter, diced

20 g (4 oz) brown sugar

Preheat the oven to 180°C (350°F), gas mark 4.

Place the quinces in a saucepan with a little water and the sugar. Simmer gently for 10 minutes.

Add the apples and pears to the saucepan and simmer for a further 5 minutes. Remove from the heat and add the essence of rosewater.

Prepare the crumble topping by putting the flour and butter into a bowl and rubbing them together lightly with your finger tips to form large crumbs. Add the sugar and mix well to disperse evenly.

Place the fruit in an ovenproof dish and sprinkle over the crumble topping.

Bake in the preheated oven for about 25 minutes, until the topping is golden brown.

Serve with thick crème fraîche or custard.

Morello cherry crumble

filling

450 g (1lb) drained weight canned or bottled Morello cherries, pitted

1 tablespoon ground rice or tapioca

topping

120 g (4 oz) plain flour

pinch of salt

120 g (4 oz) unsalted butter, diced

120 g (4 oz) caster sugar

120 g (4 oz) ground hazelnuts

Preheat the oven to 180°C (350°F), gas mark 4.

Prepare the crumble topping by putting the flour, salt and butter into a bowl and rubbing them together lightly with your finger tips to form large crumbs. Stir in the sugar and the ground hazelnuts and mix well to disperse evenly. Allow to stand in the refrigerator.

Mix the cherries with the ground rice or tapioca. Spread evenly in an ovenproof dish.

Spread the topping evenly over the cherry filling.

Bake in the preheated oven for around 30 minutes, until golden brown.

Serve lightly dusted with cinnamon-flavoured icing sugar or with praline-flavoured ice cream.

Spicy pear crumble

filling

6 pears, peeled, cored and quartered

50 g (2 oz) unsalted butter

topping

3 slices of pain d'épice, or other spiced loaf, or gingerbread

5 ginger thins or other spiced biscuits

70 g (3 oz) unsalted butter, diced

100 g (3½ oz) plain flour

Note: Williams pears are good for this, or use firm eating pears

Preheat the oven to 180°C (350°F), gas mark 4.

Brown the pears in the butter over a high heat.

Break up the spiced loaf or gingerbread slices and the biscuits into crumbs in a food processor. Add the butter and flour and process until the mixture resembles large breadcrumbs. Place the pears in an ovenproof dish and cover with the crumble topping.

Bake in the preheated oven for around 20 minutes, until the topping is golden brown.

Serve with creamy yogurt or honey-flavoured ice cream.

Black fruit crumble

filling

800 g (1⅓ lb) dark plums, pitted

50 g (2 oz) caster sugar

600 g (1¼ lb) figs, peeled and cut into quarters

200 g (7 oz) blackberries

topping

150 g (5 oz) plain flour

pinch of salt

100 g (3½ oz) unsalted butter, diced

80 g (3 oz) Demerara sugar

1 teaspoon cinnamon

Preheat the oven to 180°C (350°F), gas mark 4.

Simmer the plums in a saucepan with the sugar and a little water for 5 minutes. Remove the pan from the heat and add the figs and blackberries.

Prepare the crumble topping by putting the flour, salt and butter into a bowl and rubbing them together lightly with your finger tips to form large crumbs. Add the sugar and cinnamon and mix well to disperse evenly.

Spread the fruit evenly in an ovenproof dish, sprinkle over the crumble topping.

Bake in the preheated oven for around 30 minutes, until topping is golden brown.

Serve with whipped cream.

Lemon crumble

filling

240 ml (8 fl oz) lemon juice

rind from 2 lemons

125 g (4 oz) caster sugar

60 g (2½ oz) unsalted
butter, diced

4 eggs

450 g (14 oz) natural yogurt

4 teaspoons cornflour

topping

160 g (5½ oz) plain flour

pinch of salt

90 g (3½ oz) unsalted
butter, diced

60 g (2½ oz) caster sugar

Preheat the oven to 160°C (325°F), gas mark 3.

Place the lemon juice and rind in a bowl with the sugar, butter
and eggs and heat over a pan of barely simmering water, or in
a double boiler, to thicken, stirring continuously until smooth.

Mix the yogurt and cornflour together and add to the lemon
mixture. Pour into a porcelain ovenproof dish.

Prepare the crumble topping by putting the flour, salt and
butter into a bowl and rubbing them together lightly with
your finger tips to form large crumbs. Add the sugar and
mix well to disperse evenly.

Sprinkle the crumble gently over the lemon mixture so that it
stays on the surface without sinking in.

Bake on the top shelf of the preheated oven for 35–40
minutes, until the lemon mixture and the crumble are
glazed and well blended.

Serve warm.

Quick red fruit crumble

filling

200 ml (7 fl oz) whipping cream, chilled for at least 1 hour

15 g (½ oz) vanilla sugar, or icing sugar with vanilla essence to taste

700 g (1½ lb) mixed red fruit

topping

8 small (very crumbly) shortbread biscuits

Whip the cream, adding the vanilla sugar halfway through.

Divide the fruit between six small ramekins and top with the whipped cream.

At the last moment, crumble the shortbread biscuits and sprinkle over each ramekin. Keep refrigerated until ready to serve, but not for too long or the biscuit crumbs will go soft.

Nectarine crumble

filling

1.2 kg (2$\frac{1}{2}$ lb) nectarines or just-ripened yellow peaches, peeled and sliced into eighths.

1 teaspoon essence of orange flower water

topping

150 g (5 oz) plain flour

pinch of salt

100 g (3$\frac{1}{2}$ oz) unsalted butter, diced

120 g (4 oz) caster sugar

100 g (3$\frac{1}{2}$ oz) pistachio nuts, roughly chopped

a few drops of almond essence

Preheat the oven to 180°C (350°F), gas mark 4.

Arrange the nectarines in an ovenproof dish and flavour with the essence of orange flower water.

Prepare the crumble topping by putting the flour, salt and butter into a bowl and rubbing them together lightly with your finger tips to form large crumbs. Stir in the sugar, pistachio nuts and almond essence and mix well to disperse evenly.

Sprinkle the topping over the nectarine filling.

Bake in the preheated oven for around 30 minutes, until the topping is golden brown.

Serve warm or cold.

English summer crumble

filling

500 g (1 lb) rhubarb, cut into chunks

500 g (1 lb) strawberries, halved or quartered (depending on size)

2 bananas, sliced

40 g (1½ oz) caster sugar

topping

120 g (4 oz) plain flour

pinch of salt

100 g (3½ oz) unsalted butter, diced

100 g (3½ oz) caster sugar

80 g (3 oz) desiccated coconut

Preheat the oven to 180°C (350°F), gas mark 4.

Place the prepared fruit in an ovenproof dish and sprinkle with the sugar.

Prepare the crumble topping by putting the flour, salt and butter into a bowl and rubbing them together lightly with your finger tips to form large crumbs. Add the sugar and mix well to disperse evenly. Stir in the coconut.

Sprinkle the crumble mixture over the fruit filling.

Bake in the preheated oven for 30–40 minutes, until the topping is golden brown.

Tropical crumble

filling

5 passion fruits

2 just-ripe mangoes, peeled and cut into pieces

50 g (2 oz) caster sugar

rind and juice of 1 lime

10 basil leaves, finely chopped

topping

150 g (5 oz) plain flour

pinch of salt

100 g (3½ oz) unsalted butter, diced

80 g (3 oz) caster sugar

3 sponge fingers, crushed

4 tablespoons toasted coconut shavings

Preheat the oven to 180°C (350°F), gas mark 4.

Cut open the passion fruits, remove the flesh and pass through a fine sieve to extract the juice.

Place the mangoes in a shallow dish and add the sugar, lime rind, juice and basil. Marinate in the refrigerator for 2–3 hours.

Prepare the crumble topping by putting the flour, salt and butter into a bowl and rubbing them together lightly with your finger tips to form large crumbs. Add the sugar and mix well to disperse evenly.

Place the marinated fruit at the bottom of an ovenproof dish and cover with the crushed sponge fingers followed by the crumble topping. Bake in the preheated oven for 30–35 minutes, until golden brown.

Decorate with the coconut shavings and serve with your favourite sorbet.

Spicy crumble

filling

1 orange

1 kg (2 lbs) red plums, pitted

250 g (8 oz) prunes, pitted

2 cloves

1 cinnamon stick
(or ½ tablespoon ground cinnamon)

1 piece of fresh root ginger, peeled and grated
(or ½ tablespoon ground ginger)

topping

150 g (5 oz) plain flour

100 g (3½ oz) ground almonds

pinch of salt

125 g (4 oz) unsalted butter, diced

100 g (3½ oz) dark Muscovado sugar
(or Demerara sugar)

Preheat the oven to 180°C (350°F), gas mark 4.

Wash the orange and remove a strip of the rind with a vegetable peeler. Squeeze the juice.

Place the plums, prunes, spices, orange juice and strip of rind in a pan. Add a little water and simmer for 15 minutes.

Prepare the crumble topping by putting the flour, ground almonds, salt and butter into a bowl and rubbing them together lightly with your finger tips to form large crumbs. Add the sugar and mix well to disperse evenly.

Remove the fresh spices and orange rind from the stewed fruit and pour into an ovenproof dish. Spread the crumble over the top.

Bake in the preheated oven for 20 minutes, until the topping is golden brown.

Serve with soured cream or creamy yogurt.

Cheesecake crumble

filling

4 eggs

100 g (3½ oz) caster sugar

1 teaspoon vanilla essence, or finely grated rind from 1 lemon

6 baby pots natural fromage frais (petits suisse), (or 360g/12 oz natural full-fat fromage frais)

300g (10 oz) soft cream cheese

topping

12 small butter biscuits, crushed

3 tablespoons rolled oats

50g (2oz) butter, melted

1 tablespoon brown sugar

pinch of salt

Preheat the oven to 120°C (250°F), gas mark ½.

Beat the eggs with the sugar until light and fluffy. Add the vanilla essence, fromage frais and cream cheese.

Pour the mixture into an ovenproof porcelain dish.

Bake in the preheated oven for 45–50 minutes, until the centre is firm to the touch.

Turn off the oven and leave the cheesecake in the oven until it is quite cold. Remove from oven and refrigerate for at least 2 hours or preferably overnight.

Prepare the crumble topping by mixing all the ingredients lightly together. Spread the topping over the cheesecake, pressing lightly, then leave in the refrigerator until ready to serve.

Serve with a red fruit coulis.

Apricot and lavender crumble

filling

40 g (1½ oz) unsalted butter

1.2 kg (2½ lb) apricots, pitted and quartered

100 g (3½ oz) caster sugar

2 or 3 drops of essential lavender oil

topping

150 g (5 oz) plain flour

pinch of salt

120 g (4 oz) unsalted butter, diced

120 g (4 oz) caster sugar

40 g (1½ oz) flaked almonds

Preheat the oven to 180°C (350°F), gas mark 4.

Melt the butter in a large frying pan over a high heat and add the apricots. Sprinkle with sugar and continue cooking until the fruit is glazed.

Remove from the heat, add the essential lavender oil and then pour the apricots into an ovenproof dish.

Prepare the crumble topping by putting the flour, salt and butter into a bowl and rubbing them together lightly with your finger tips to form large crumbs. Add the sugar and mix well to disperse evenly.

Spread the crumble topping over the apricots and sprinkle with the flaked almonds.

Bake in the preheated oven for 25–30 minutes. Serve warm.

Sweet spiced tomato crumble

filling

1 kg (2 lbs) firm tomatoes, skinned, deseeded and chopped

1 mango, peeled and chopped

40 g (1½ oz) unsalted butter

2 tablespoons caster sugar

1 small piece of fresh root ginger, peeled and grated

a few crushed green peppercorns, fresh or dried (or a few turns of a peppermill of freeze-dried green peppercorns)

seeds scraped from 1 vanilla pod

topping

150 g (5 oz) plain flour

pinch of salt

100 g (3½ oz) butter, diced

80 g (3 oz) caster sugar

Preheat the oven to 180°C (350°F), gas mark 4.

Brown the tomatoes and mango in the butter over a high heat. Sprinkle with sugar and cook until well glazed.

Remove from the heat and add the ginger, crushed or ground green peppercorns and the seeds from the vanilla pod. Pour into an ovenproof dish.

Prepare the crumble topping by putting the flour, salt and butter into a bowl and rubbing them together lightly with your finger tips to form large crumbs. Add the sugar and mix well to disperse evenly.

Bake on the top shelf of the preheated oven for 15–20 minutes.

Serve warm with well-chilled single cream or a scoop of vanilla ice cream.

Winter fruit crumble

filling

2 teaspoons loose leaf tea (Earl Grey, Lapsang Souchong or jasmine tea are good)

100 g (3½ oz) prunes, pitted

100 g (3½ oz) dried apricots

100 g (3½ oz) dried pears

80 g (3 oz) large sweet seedless raisins

topping

180 g (6 oz) plain whole-meal flour

pinch of salt

80 g (3 oz) unsalted butter, diced

60 g (2½ oz) Demerara or dark Muscovado sugar

1 tablespoon toasted sesame oil

2 tablespoons toasted sesame seeds

The night before: make 1 litre (1¾ pints) of tea and use to soak the prunes and the other dried fruit overnight.

The following day: preheat the oven to 180°C (350°F), gas mark 4.

Prepare the crumble topping by putting the flour, salt and butter into a bowl and rubbing them together lightly with your finger tips to form large crumbs. Add the sugar, sesame oil and seeds and mix well to disperse evenly.

Strain the fruit, keeping a little of the marinade, and cut into pieces if required.

Place the fruit in an ovenproof dish, adding a little of the reserved juice if needed, and sprinkle over the crumble topping evenly.

Bake in the preheated oven for around 30 minutes, until the topping is golden brown.

Serve with soured cream or fromage frais.

Dark chocolate crumble

filling

250 ml (8 fl oz) single cream

100 ml (3½ fl oz) milk

200 g (8 oz) dark chocolate (minimum 70% solids), grated

1 whole egg plus 3 egg yolks, beaten

topping

75 g (3 oz) roasted hazelnuts

75 g (3 oz) caster sugar

100 g (3½ oz) plain flour

pinch of salt

75 g (3 oz) unsalted butter, diced

Preheat the oven to 120°C (250°F), gas mark ½.

Prepare the crumble topping by putting the hazelnuts and the sugar in a small pan over moderate heat. When the sugar begins to melt and caramelize, remove from the heat. Mix together in a food processor, adding the flour, salt and finally the butter, taking care not to over-work the mixture.

Put the cream and milk into a pan and bring gently to the boil. Remove from the heat and add the grated chocolate. Leave to stand for 5 minutes and then mix until thoroughly blended.

Add the beaten eggs to the chocolate mixture, which should thicken and take on the consistency of mayonnaise.

Pour the chocolate mixture into an ovenproof dish and spread over the crumble topping very gently.

Bake on the top shelf of the preheated oven for 40 minutes. Then place under a preheated grill until the topping is golden brown, taking care not to let it burn.

Serve warm or cold.

White chocolate crumble

filling

3 dessert apples, preferably pippins, peeled, cored and sliced

4 bananas, sliced

3 tablespoons raisins, soaked in rum

topping

60 g (2½ oz) white chocolate (coconut flavour if possible)

100 g (3½ oz) plain flour

pinch of salt

100 g (3½ oz) unsalted butter, diced

70 g (3 oz) caster sugar

100 g (3½ oz) grated coconut

½ tablespoon ground cinnamon

Preheat the oven to 180°C (350°F), gas mark 4.

Break up the white chocolate coarsely in a food processor or chop into very small pieces.

Prepare the crumble topping by putting the flour, salt and butter into a bowl and rubbing them together lightly with your finger tips to form large crumbs. Stir in the sugar, coconut and cinnamon. Allow to stand in the refrigerator for 2 hours.

Soften the apples in a saucepan for 10 minutes, with just sufficient water so that the apples do not stick. Remove from the heat, add the banana slices and the raisins and pour the fruit into an ovenproof dish.

Mix the chopped white chocolate into the crumble topping and sprinkle over the fruit.

Bake in the preheated oven for around 30 minutes.

Serve with custard.

Pear, banana and chocolate crumble

filling

5 pears, peeled, cored and diced

2 bananas, sliced

25 g (1 oz) crystallized ginger, finely chopped

topping

100 g (3½ oz) plain flour

100 g (3½ oz) unsalted butter, diced

60 g (2½ oz) ground almonds

100 g (3½ oz) caster sugar

2 tablespoons cocoa powder

1 teaspoon ground ginger

100 g (3½ oz) chocolate chips

Preheat the oven to 180°C (350°F), gas mark 4.

Place the pears and bananas in an ovenproof dish along with the crystallized ginger.

Prepare the crumble topping by putting the flour and butter into a bowl and rubbing them together lightly with your finger tips until the mixture is the consistency of fine breadcrumbs. Stir in the ground almonds, sugar, cocoa powder, ground ginger and the chocolate chips.

Spread the topping over the fruit.

Bake in the preheated oven for around 20 minutes.

Serve warm with your favourite sorbet.

Iced coffee crumble

filling

300 ml (½ pint) milk

2 teaspoons freeze-dried instant coffee

60 g (2½ oz) caster sugar

3 egg yolks

300 ml (½ pint) whipping cream, chilled for at least 1 hour

topping

50 g (2 oz) shelled walnuts

40 g (1½ oz) thin butter biscuits (e.g. almond thins)

1 teaspoon freeze-dried instant coffee

Place the milk in a pan with 1 teaspoon of the instant coffee and warm over gentle heat. At the same time, beat the sugar and egg yolks together until light and frothy. Pour in the warm milk and continue to beat. Pour the mixture into a pan and cook over gentle heat to thicken, stirring continuously, taking care not to let the mixture boil. Remove from the heat and allow to cool, stirring occasionally to speed up the cooling process.

Whip the cream as for Chantilly cream (see page 4) and allow to stand in the refrigerator.

Blend the walnuts and biscuits in a food processor or blender until they resemble fine breadcrumbs. Add the coffee. Divide this mixture into small individual ramekins.

When the coffee cream mixture is cool, mix carefully with the Chantilly cream. Finally, add the remaining teaspoon of coffee and divide the mousse between the ramekins. Freeze for a minimum of 3 hours, removing from the freezer at least 10 minutes before serving.

Savoury tomato crumble

filling

30 g (1oz) butter

1 tablespoon brown sugar

250 g (8 oz) small white onions, peeled and quartered

1.2 kg (2½ lb) plum (or round) tomatoes skinned, deseeded and cut into quarters

pinch thyme

pinch rosemary

salt and pepper

topping

100 g (4 oz) plain flour

pinch of salt

80 g (3 oz) butter, diced

60 g (2½ oz) roasted hazelnuts, crushed

40 g (1½ oz) Parmesan cheese

1 tablespoon olive oil

Preheat the oven to 180°C (350°F), gas mark 4.

Melt the butter and brown sugar together over low heat in an oven-and-flameproof dish, then brown the onions.

Place the tomatoes in a sieve and shake off the liquid until they are well drained. Once the onions are cooked, arrange the tomatoes on top and season with the herbs and salt and pepper to taste.

Prepare the crumble topping by putting the flour, salt and butter into a bowl and rubbing them together lightly with your finger tips to form large crumbs. Stir in the hazelnuts, Parmesan and olive oil and mix well together.

Spread the crumble topping over the tomatoes and bake in the preheated oven for 30 minutes, until golden brown.

Serve with fresh goats' cheese, mashed with a fork and mixed with a little whipped cream.

Courgette crumble

filling

1 kg (2 lb) courgettes, cleaned, trimmed and finely grated

2 tablespoons fine semolina

250 g (8 oz) fresh goats' cheese, diced

½ bunch of mint leaves, chopped

salt and pepper

topping

150 g (5 oz) plain wholemeal flour

pinch of salt

75 g (3 oz) butter, diced

2 teaspoons olive oil

Preheat the oven to 180°C (350°F), gas mark 4.

Squeeze the grated courgettes by hand to make sure all the juice is extracted. Sprinkle with the semolina.

Roughly mix the goats' cheese and chopped mint with the courgettes and spread the mixture in an ovenproof dish. Season to taste.

Prepare the crumble topping by putting the flour, salt and butter into a bowl and rubbing them together lightly with your finger tips, adding the olive oil until the mixture resembles coarse semolina (a little extra oil might be needed to make the topping seem less dry).

Spread the crumble topping over the courgettes and bake in the preheated oven for 20–25 minutes, or until golden brown.

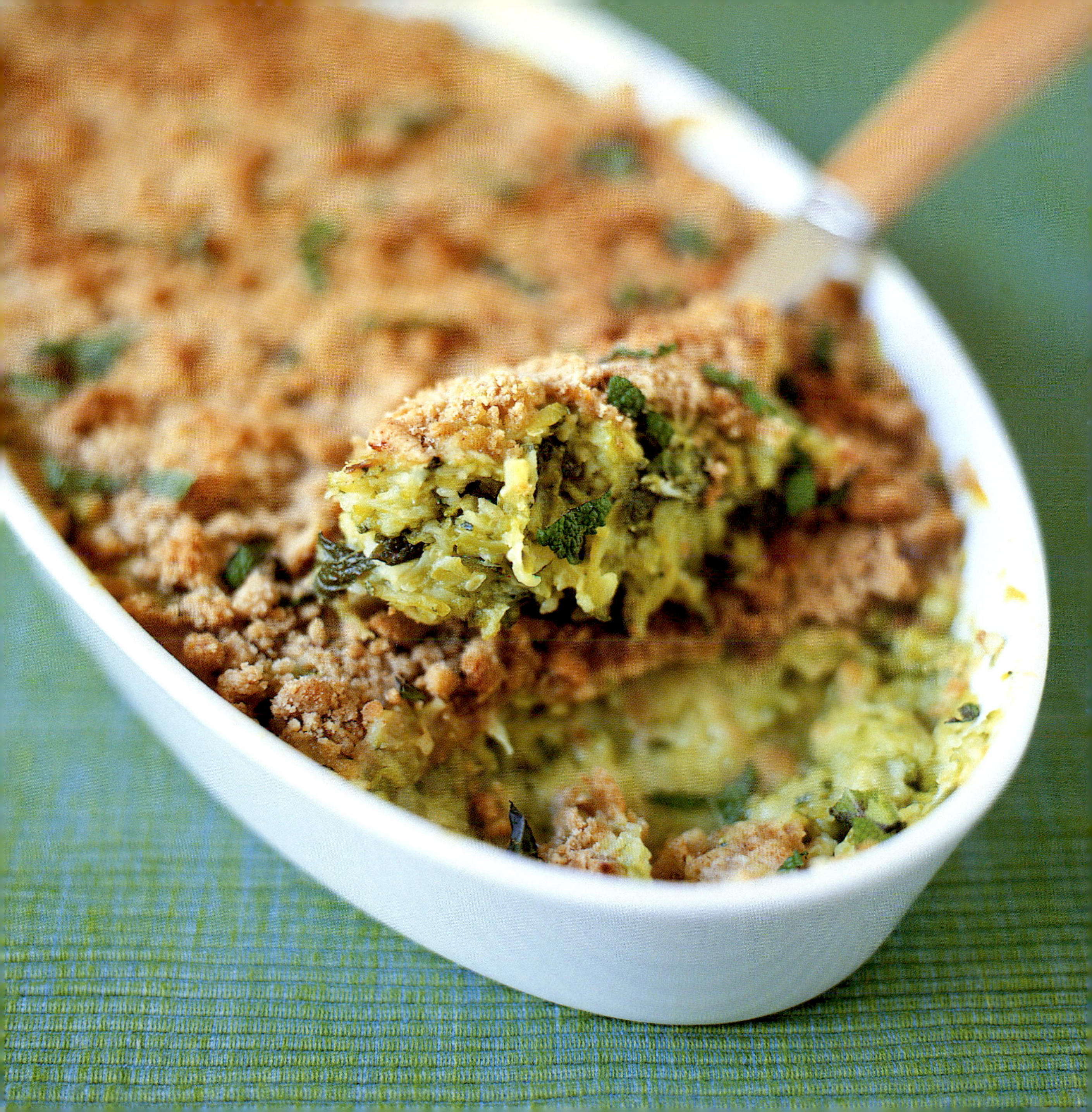

Pumpkin crumble

filling

1 kg (2 lbs) pumpkin, peeled and cut into large cubes

2 onions, thinly sliced

2 sage leaves, finely chopped

100 g (3½ oz) bacon or thinly sliced smoked ham, cut into fine strips

1 tablespoon crème fraîche

150 g (5 oz) Cheddar cheese, cut into small dice

topping

150 g (5oz) plain wholemeal flour

80 g (3 oz) butter, diced

80 g (3 oz) Cheddar cheese, cut into small dice

Preheat the oven to 180°C (350°F), gas mark 4.

Place the pumpkin, onion and sage into an ovenproof dish. Add a few drops of water and place in the preheated oven for about 30–40 minutes or until the pumpkin can be mashed with a fork.

While the pumpkin mixture is cooking, prepare the crumble topping by putting the flour and butter into a bowl and rubbing them together lightly with your finger tips to form large crumbs. Add the 80 g (3 oz) of Cheddar.

Remove the dish from the oven, roughly mash the pumpkin and add the bacon, crème fraîche and the remaining 150 g (5 oz) of Cheddar.

Spread the crumble topping over the pumpkin mixture and bake for a further 20 minutes until the crust is golden brown.

Spring vegetable crumble

filling

1 kg (2 lbs) mixed baby or young vegetables (carrots, courgettes, mushrooms, leeks, peas, green beans)

300 ml (½ pint) single cream

100 g (4 oz) streaky bacon, cut into small ribbons

a few sprigs of chives, chervil and tarragon, finely chopped

topping

100 g (3½ oz) plain flour

100 g (3½ oz) butter, diced

50 g (2 oz) breadcrumbs

Preheat the oven to 180°C (350°F), gas mark 4.

Grate the carrots and courgettes, finely chop the mushrooms and cut the leeks into thin slices. Blanch the peas and green beans for 2–3 minutes in salted boiling water. Drain.

Prepare the crumble topping by putting the flour and butter into a bowl and rubbing them together lightly with your finger tips to form large crumbs. Stir in the breadcrumbs.

Mix the vegetables with the cream, bacon and chopped herbs. Pour into an ovenproof dish and cover with the crumble topping.

Bake in the preheated oven for 30–40 minutes, until golden.

Mediterranean crumble

ratatouille filling

3 tablespoons olive oil

1 onion, sliced

1 garlic clove, finely chopped

1 good-sized aubergine, cut into small cubes

1 red pepper and 1 green pepper, cut into strips

sprigs of thyme and rosemary

salt and pepper

3 nicely firm courgettes, cut into round slices

1 kg (2 lbs) tomatoes, skinned and deseeded

topping

150 g (5 oz) plain flour

pinch of salt

100 g (3½ oz) butter, diced

60 g (2½ oz) grated Parmesan cheese

40 g (1½ oz) pine nuts

Preheat the oven to 180°C (350°F), gas mark 4.

Heat the oil in an ovenproof casserole over moderate heat and brown the onion and garlic together.

Add the aubergine. When it is well browned, add the peppers and season with a little chopped thyme and rosemary, salt and pepper. Cook for 20 minutes, then add the courgettes and tomatoes. Mix well and continue to simmer fairly vigorously so that the vegetables give up their juice.

Meanwhile, prepare the crumble topping by putting the flour, salt and butter into a bowl and rubbing them together lightly with your finger tips to form large crumbs. Stir in the Parmesan and the pine nuts.

Pour the ratatouille into an ovenproof dish and spread over the crumble topping.

Bake in the preheated oven for 20–30 minutes, until golden brown.

Serve hot with fresh goats' cheese or thin slices of mozzarella.

Crumble Indian style

filling

200 g (7 oz) carrots, sliced into small sticks

200 g (7 oz) shelled peas

200 g (7 oz) red or green pepper, cut into small cubes

200 g (8 oz) cauliflower, cut in small florets

1 teaspoon curry powder

150 ml (¼ pint) single cream

10 triangles of 'Laughing Cow' cheese (or about 175 g/6 oz spreadable cheese), cut into small pieces

salt

topping

150 g (5 oz) plain flour

pinch of salt

80 g (3 oz) unsalted butter, diced

80 g (3 oz) cashew nuts, roughly chopped

sauce

450 g (15 oz) full-fat natural yogurt

½ bunch of fresh coriander, chopped

a few drops of lemon juice

pinch salt

Preheat the oven to 180°C (350°F), gas mark 4.

Blanch the vegetables in salted boiling water for 5 minutes and then drain, reserving a little cooking water in case you need to 'loosen' the filling. Season the vegetables with the curry powder, then add the cream and soft cheese. Transfer to a porcelain ovenproof dish.

Prepare the crumble topping by putting the flour, salt and butter into a bowl and rubbing them together lightly with your finger tips to form large crumbs. Stir in the cashew nuts.

Sprinkle the topping over the vegetables and bake in the preheated oven for around 20–30 minutes.

Meanwhile prepare the sauce by mixing the yogurt, coriander and lemon juice together and seasoning to taste. Chill until required.

Serve the crumble warm with the chilled sauce.

Oriental crumble

filling

1.2 kg (2½ lb) spinach, cleaned, trimmed and cut into strips

1 teaspoon olive oil

3 tablespoons thick crème fraîche

150 g (5 oz) feta cheese

3 tablespoons currants

2 tablespoons pine nuts

pinch of nutmeg

topping

2 tablespoons olive oil

150 g (5 oz) plain flour

pinch of salt

50 g (2 oz) butter, diced

70 g (3 oz) feta cheese, mashed with a fork

1 teaspoon ground cinnamon

Preheat the oven to 180°C (350°F), gas mark 4.

Pour the olive oil to be used for the topping into a bowl and place in the freezer.

Fry the spinach in the teaspoon of oil. Once it is tender and has given up all its liquid, add the crème fraîche, feta cheese, currants and pine nuts. Season with nutmeg and place in an ovenproof dish.

Prepare the crumble by putting the flour, salt, butter and hardened oil into a bowl and rubbing them together with the finger tips to form large crumbs. Mix in the mashed feta cheese.

Spread the mixture over the filling and sprinkle with ground cinnamon. Bake in the preheated oven for 20 minutes.

Moroccan crumble

filling

250 g (8 oz) artichoke
hearts, sliced

250 g (8 oz) potatoes,
cut in to large dice

500 g (1 lb) courgettes,
peeled and cut in to
2.5-cm (1-inch) slices

20 green olives, pitted
and halved

1/4 preserved lemon,
cut into small pieces

2 tablespoons salted
capers, rinsed

1 garlic clove, split in half

10 sprigs of fresh coriander,
chopped

1 teaspoon ras-el-hanout
(Moroccan mixed spices)

2 tablespoons lemon juice

100 ml (3 1/2 fl oz) water

topping

2 sheets of filo pastry,
or 8 sheets of brick (light
Moroccan pastry), cut into
strips with scissors

4 tablespoons olive oil

Preheat the oven to 160°C (325°F), gas mark 3.

Put the vegetables into an ovenproof dish. Add the olives, preserved lemon, capers, garlic, half the chopped coriander and the ras-el-hanout spice. Pour in the lemon juice and measured water.

Cover with aluminium foil and bake in the preheated oven for around 1 hour until the vegetables are tender.

Remove the garlic and add the remaining freshly chopped coriander and keep warm.

Heat a little oil in a frying pan and fry the strips of filo (or brick) in small batches, until crisp and brown.

Crumble the crispy filo strips with your fingers over the vegetables and keep the dish warm until ready to serve.

Note: If using brick, take care that the fried strips do not go soft.

Chicken liver crumble

filling

500 g (1 lb) celeriac, peeled, quartered, and thinly sliced

350 g (12 oz) chicken livers, rinsed, connecting strings removed, leaving the lobes separated

2–3 tablespoons unsalted butter

2 sharp dessert apples (Braeburn or pippin), peeled, cored and finely diced

300 g (10 oz) (final weight) pears, peeled, cored and finely diced

salt and black pepper

topping

150 g (5 oz) plain flour

pinch of salt

70 g (3 oz) unsalted butter

50 g (2 oz) chopped walnuts

Preheat the oven to 180°C (350°F), gas mark 4.

Prepared the crumble by putting the flour, salt and butter into a bowl and rubbing them together lightly with your finger tips to form large crumbs. Stir in the walnuts. Set aside in the refrigerator.

Blanch the slices of celeriac in boiling water for 5 minutes. Drain thoroughly.

Pat dry the prepared chicken livers with kitchen paper. Melt half the butter in a frying pan over a moderate heat, add half the livers in a single layer and cook undisturbed for 1 minute, turn them over and cook for a further 1–2 minutes until firm, but do not over cook. Set aside and cook the remaining livers, adding more butter if needed.

Place the chicken livers in an ovenproof dish, or in individual rings on a baking sheet. Cover with layers of apple and pear, seasoning between each layer. Top with slices of celariac.

Spread the crumble topping over the celeriac slices and bake in the preheated oven for about 20–25 minutes. Check that the chicken livers are cooked and, if necessary, brown the topping under a preheated grill. Serve with a green salad.

Note: Alternatively, you can make this recipe using foie gras. Replace the chicken livers with 1 lobe of raw foie gras, about 350-400 g (11-13 oz), cut into strips. Lay the strips in an ovenproof dish and top with the fruit and celeriac, seasoning between each layer. Sprinkle with the crumble topping and bake in the preheated oven for 25–30 minutes, taking care that the crust does not brown too quickly. Make sure that the foie gras is cooked before serving; if necessary, cook for longer.

Acknowledgements
Bernardaud (chinaware)
Conran Shop (linen, crockery and cutlery)
Kitchen Bazar (cutlery and crockery)

© Marabout 2002
text and design © Camille Le Foll
photographs © Akiko Ida

© Hachette 2001
This edition © 2003 Hachette Illustrated UK, Octopus Publishing Group,
2–4 Heron Quays, London E14 4JP
English translation by JMS Books LLP (email: moseleystrachan@blueyonder.co.uk)
Translation © Octopus Publishing Group

A CIP catalogue for this book is available from the British Library

ISBN: 1 84430 030 7

Printed by Tien Wah Press, Singapore